To Ry____

From ____

x

Other books in this series:
HAPPY ANNIVERSARY
To a very special AUNT
To someone special, celebrating your
    LOVELY NEW BABY
To a very special DAUGHTER
To a very special FRIEND
To a very special GRANDDAUGHTER
To a very special GRANDMA
To a very special GRANDPA

To a very special GRANDSON
Wishing you HAPPINESS
To my very special HUSBAND
Someone very special…
    TO THE ONE I LOVE
To a very special MOTHER
To a very special SISTER
To a very special TEACHER
To my very special WIFE

Published in 1993 by Helen Exley Giftbooks in Great Britain.
This revised edition published in 2008

12 11 10 9 8 7 6 5 4 3 2

ISBN 13: 978-1-84634-287-5

To our own very special sons Lincoln and Dalton and Colin and Max, to say the
things they won't allow us to say aloud.

Helen Exley Giftbooks, 16 Chalk Hill, Watford, Herts WD19 4BG, UK.
www.helenexleygiftbooks.com

To a very special®
SON

ILLUSTRATIONS BY JULIETTE CLARKE.
WRITTEN BY PAM BROWN.
EDITED BY HELEN EXLEY.

I am here for you always –
proud of you, believing in
you, and hoping
your dreams come true.

HELEN EXLEY®

HAPPINESS IS A SON

Sons teach you how to laugh again.
Loudly.

When nothing's gone right all day and you're
feeling the weight of every failure,
it only needs the rush of small feet pounding
down the path, a leap, arms locked about
you, a grin, a pouring out of the day's news
– and everything goes your way.

Even if a son is in and out of the
house in ten minutes flat, he leaves
behind him a great swirl of fresh air.

However hard the day has been,
the smiling face of a
small son pressed against a window pane
is a sure-fire remedy.

Parents don't know perfect happiness
until they've swung their small
child high in the air – shouting with joy!

A son is the biggest bonus life can offer.

Every mother
cries silently to
her sons – be
bold, be brave –
but be very,
very, careful!

A SON IS...

– the one who believes that if it's in the refrigerator
it's there to be eaten.

– someone who regards you as an amiable idiot -
but loves you all the same.

– the softie who gives you a gorgeous gift in a tatty
plastic bag, with the price label still on it.

– the one who regards you as the totally reliable
source of shirts.

– the amiable one who wants to do everything
for you. It's just getting round to it.

– the guy who flings himself. He bounces, bumps,
ducks, dives, slides, pounds, paddles, fidgets
and falls. Then he picks himself up and does
it all again.
– the one who cheerfully lets himself in at 3:00 a.m.
all set to tell you what a wonderful time he's
had. And is hurt and astounded to find you don't
want to know.
– the voice who reverses the telephone charges from
Bangkok and says he knows you will not mind.
(Which, of course, you don't.)
– the young man pulling his motorbike apart in the
kitchen because it's raining.
– the fellow with all the friends that you find
sleeping on the living room floor.
– the boy who says things that drive
his parents to the edge – but smiles at exactly
the right moment.

THANK YOU FOR EVERYTHING

Thank you for putting exclamation marks in my life

Thank you for the cups of cold tea when you were
very small ("I found it in the pot"). Thank you for
the fluff-covered toffees donated from your pocket.
Thank you for the peppermint-tasting kisses.
Thank you for drawings, and the messages of love.
Thank you for the ice-cold cuddles in the dead of a
winter's night. Thank you for naming your
hamster after me. Thank you for
love greater than I've ever deserved.

Thank you for all your gifts – all your kindnesses.
Like the dead frog and the wilting dandelions and
the mud puddings.
Like the tie-dye scarf and the clay elephant.
Like the pond you dug, lined, filled and planted
when I'd been lured to see friends for the day.
All of them treasured still.

Son – thank you for getting under my feet, causing
me sleepless nights, costing me a small fortune,
interfering with my plans. What on earth would I
have done with my time without you?

GROWING PAINS

Small sons should be patented as dirt collectors.
It is a proven fact that paint, glue, mud,
soot, oil, ink, jam, scum and ketchup will leap
considerable distances to adhere to them.
The difficulty is removing the dirt
from the dirt collectors.
No soap or scourer has yet been invented
that will completely clean a small son.
Thankfully, grime usually wears off after a few years

A head comes round the door. A worried face.
A staccato of blown kisses. What has he dropped?
What has he smashed? What has he torn?
"It's all right, Love. It can't be as bad as that.
Come and tell me." He has the pieces in his hand.
"I didn't ackcherly do it. It sort of slipped.
And there it was. Broke. I'm *sorry*".
Ah, well. Boys are more precious than possessions.

Sons, as they grow older, are inclined to be horribly
embarrassed by their parents. They forget the times
they had their hair shaved, retreated under
the table in restaurants, sang off-key at Karaoke,
shouted during solemn ceremonies.

Almost all sons go through a Bad Patch,
when their parents would cheerfully trade
them in. Thankfully, they usually grow out of it
just before any deal is struck.

EVERYONE SHOULD HAVE A SON...

to give them a cheerful grin when the world is drab.

to praise their cooking when it's not that wonderful.

– to give them unexpected hugs.

– to bring home surprises – frogs, electronic gizmos,
girlfriends with green hair.

– to lure them into adventures ("You'll love it, Dad.
Pull the ripcord and there you are....")

– to widen their minds ("OK – so it's hip-hop.
Just let the music sink into your *bones*.")

– to increase their circle of friends ("This is Bob,
Ma. He's a Rastafarian.")

– to stimulate their brains ("But I have to know by
tomorrow, in detail, what was Mithraism?")

– to sharpen their vocabulary ("Do that just once
more, Son, and I'll....")

– to teach them patience ("I'll do it later,
I swear I will. After I've done this.")

– to love.

PROUD OF YOU

"My son" – the happiest introduction.

A mother's proudest boast of any of her sons
is not his wealth or his success – but that he is
a good son, a good friend. A decent person.

Parents glow a little when people say
"Isn't he handsome? Isn't he charming?
Hasn't he done well?"
But they treasure forever "Isn't he kind?",
"He always remembers...",
"I'd trust him with my life."

It will make me deeply, quietly proud
of you if you can stay the same and
kind and caring in a world where such
things seem less important than projecting
the Right Image. In my eyes you will have
succeeded if you're not spoken of
with awe or fear or envy
– but with affection and with respect.

Parents are very proud if they produce geniuses.
Or astounding, whirlwind celebrities,
who are mobbed and quoted and photographed.
But they're rather relieved if they haven't!

I wish I could ensure you good health,
talent, wealth, a good life...
And lasting friendships, true love, satisfying
work, just recognition, adventures enough
to keep your mind and heart alive.
But I can't. No parent can.
All we do is hope – and always be
here for you.

What do I wish you? Strength.
Not necessarily of body – but of mind
and heart. Strength to endure when hope
has dwindled, when those you
thought believed in you have turned away,
when love has failed.

I wish you a mind that never ceases to learn and to wonder, the drive and energy to work for what you believe in.

I wish you love, friendships with both human beings and so-called lesser creatures, the gift of empathy, discipline of mind, joy in the mastery of some skill and boundless curiosity. I also wish you that rare ability to forgive… yourself, as well as others.

I must not dream dreams for you. Only give you the chance to dream your own. And I wish I can help you make them come true.

MISSING YOU

Sons occupy far more space
than their size would indicate.
That's why the house feels so
empty when they are gone.

The TV drama is reaching its
climax. The telephone rings.
Cursing inwardly, you reach
for the phone.
It's your son.
So who cares about who
did the murder?

Sons flash their headlights
when they leave.
It means a lot to the shadow
standing
at the window.

If parents are over-given to warnings and anxieties, it's because age has given them the high ground – and they can see where the flowery paths are leading. They care too much about you to keep their mouths shut.

There comes a time when the toys are all packed away up in the attic, when the door opens on to neatly-ordered shelves, when the laundry basket is almost empty, when the refrigerator is full. When one no longer has to step over books and bikes and legs.
And that's the time a parent needs a phone call.

I have a little addition on my list of hopes for you. It's something for me. However wise and successful and happy you become – send me an e-mail, a letter now and then.

COMING HOME AGAIN

Visiting sons still
remember where the cakes live.

There is a special smile that mothers
have when their tall, grown offspring are home.
Even for a few hours.
Utter contentment.

A son with 'flu heads home.

When a son has been away, how soon he fits
into his old place on his return.
He may not stay – but there is a renewal
in the hearts of all the family. He leaves reassured.
There is one place in the world where he can be
accepted for himself.

Even the best son will always regard his parents'
attic as an extension of his own.

Sons go far, take on many guises.
But once with the family, the uniform, the gown,
the white coat is set aside. The great world
knows sons by their achievements.
The family knows all his mistakes – all the jokes,
all the adventures, all the habits and tricks
and weaknesses of a lifetime.
Dr. Thomas Jenkins is plain Tom at home.

WHAT I'D GIVE TO YOU...
If I could choose to give you only one thing
I think it would have to be courage.
With it you could face all change,
all loss, all rejection, all failure, even loneliness.
And then build more strongly than before.

I wish you the gift of love.
Love that survives all trials and that strengthens
through the years.

The best gift any parent could give you is the gift
of clear thinking – eager, informed, disciplined,
courageous, honest, unprejudiced thought.
It sounds so very dull set against
fame and luck and phenomenal
strength – but it is far more exciting –
and leads down more important roads.

I hope with all my heart that you
become very, very good at something.
Small or large. Something.

BONDED FOREVER

Some walk away, ride away, drive away, sail away.
They always have. But the steel-strong,
web-fine links that bind them to those
who love them and whom they love in turn,
cannot be broken. Ever.

There is a comfortable kinship between sons
and their parents.
They seem to have a mysterious understanding –
and catch each other's eyes, and grin.

Sons are linked to home by invisible
unbreakable threads – forever.

When you were very small I told you
that there was a cord that held a family
together and that whatever happened it could
never snap or fray. Separation, divorce, distance
or death – it will always be there.
It stretches over any horizon. It lasts beyond any
point in our lifetimes. A reassurance,
when and if you need it.

GO, WITH MY LOVE
I do not know where you will go,
what you will do, whom you will love.
But I stand ready to applaud.

Dear Son – I like you, love you, as you are.
But I hold in my heart all the sons you've been
over the years – and like and love them all.
I share your life, and am the closer for it.

You take my love with you to places that
I will never see, to times that I will never know.
So love survives.

Do something for me, Love.
Do all the things I never was able to.
See the places I never saw.
Discover things beyond my understanding.

We hope, Son, you never need a bolt hole.
But if you do, we're it.

Of *course* I remember when you were very small.
Of course I have stored up all the things
you did and said, and will treasure them forever.
But it is you as you are that I love.
And will, however far you go, whatever brings you
down, or however much you change.
For all my life.